Airport Codes

of

North America

(and also Europe & Oceania)

by L.A. Blankenstyn

First Printing, 2019

ISBN 978-0-359-81686-6

elbee productions

Prologue

The day the airplane was invented may be regarded as a day that arguably changed the course of humanity as we know it. No longer did people have to rely on bicycles and balloons for their long-distance voyages.

…But not at first. The airplane was invented by a pair of vagrant high school dropouts known as Orville and Wilbur Wright, who took a break from their unemployment to create the world's first heavier-than-air flying machine in Kitty Hawk, North Carolina on December 1st, 1903. Being as self-centered as they were, the Wright brothers naturally kept their discovery to themselves, until January 1st, 1914, the day of the first commercial flight. Scheduled by Tony Jannus, this was a flight from St. Petersburg to Tampa. This may sound impressive, until you realise that St. Petersburg is also the name of a city in Florida, a short 24 miles away from Tampa. The flight took place in a Benoist XIV, a two-seated plane. Those seats being filled by Jannus, and one very eccentric paying customer. The flight lasted twenty-three long minutes.

Five years later, in August 1919, Hounslow Heath Aerodrome opened its doors. Here, we had the world's first airport. Hounslow Heath Aerodrome eventually proved to be a failure when it closed its doors a year later and was replaced by Croydon Airport. At least 49,024 airports have opened since then, none of which being located in the town of Kitty Hawk. More importantly, many of those airports have three letter IATA codes to identify them. These are the codes displayed on baggage tags at the airport, for the sole reason of bragging about which airport you're flying out of. This book is a further exploration of these codes. Please enjoy. (Just not too much.)

-L.A. Blankenstyn

Airport Codes of North America

USA

California ◤

Arcata/Eureka, Arcata Airport – ACV

Bakersfield, Meadows Airport – BFL

Burbank, Bob Hope Airport – BUR

Fresno Yosemite International Airport – FAT

Long Beach Airport – LGB

Los Angeles International Airport – LAX
Mammoth Lakes, Mammoth Yosemite Airport – MMH

Monterey Regional Airport – MRY

Oakland International Airport – OAK

Ontario International Airport – ONT

Palm Springs International Airport – PSP

Redding Municipal Airport – RDD

Sacramento International Airport – SMF

San Diego International Airport – SAN

San Francisco International Airport – SFO

San José, Norman Y. Mineta San José International Airport – SJC

San Luis Obispo County Regional Airport – SBP

Santa Ana, John Wayne Airport – SNA

Santa Barbara Municipal Airport – SBA

Santa Maria Public Airport – SMX

Santa Rosa, Charles M. Schulz-Sonoma County Airport – STS

Stockton Metropolitan Airport – SCK

Montana 🏴

Billings, Logan International Airport – BIL

Bozeman, Yellowstone International Airport – BZN

Butte, Bert Mooney Airport – BTM

Great Falls International Airport – GTF

Helena Regional Airport – HLN

Kalispell, Glacier Park International Airport – FCA

Missoula International Airport – MSO

Sidney-Richland Municipal Airport – SDY

Glasgow International Airport – GGW

Glendive, Dawson Community Airport – GDV

West Yellowstone, Yellowstone Airport – WYS

Wolf Point, L.M. Clayton Airport – OLF

Havre City-County Airport – HVR

WASHINGTON

Bellingham International Airport – BLI

Friday Harbor Airport – FRD

Pasco, Tri-Cities Airport – PSC

Pullman/Moscow Regional Airport – PUW

Seattle-Tacoma International Airport – SEA

Spokane International Airport – GEG

Walla Walla Regional Airport – ALW

Wenatchee, Pangborn Memorial Airport – EAT

Yakima Air Terminal – YKM

Eastsound, Orcas Island Airport – ESD

Port Angeles, William R. Fairchild International Airport – CLM

Idaho

Boise Airport – BOI

Hailey, Friedman Memorial Airport – SUN

Idaho Falls Regional Airport – IDA

Lewiston, Lewiston-Nez Perce County Airport – LWS

Pocatello Regional Airport – PIH

Twin Falls, Magic Valley Regional Airport – TWF

Oregon

Eugene Airport – EUG

Medford, Rogue Valley International-Medford Airport – MFR

North Bend, Southwest Oregon Regional Airport – OTH

Portland International Airport – PDX

Redmond Municipal Airport – RDM

Klamath Falls Airport – LMT

Pendleton, Eastern Oregon Regional Airport at Pendleton – PDT

Utah 🔲

Cedar City Regional Airport – CDC

Ogden, Ogden-Hinckley Airport – OGD

Provo Municipal Airport – PVU

Salt Lake City International Airport – SLC

St. George Regional Airport – SGU

Moab, Canyonlands Field – CNY

Vernal Regional Airport – VEL

Arizona 🔲

Bullhead City, Laughlin/Bullhead International Airport - IFP

Flagstaff Pulliam Airport – FLG

Grand Canyon National Park Airport – GCN

Mesa, Phoenix-Mesa Gateway Airport – AZA

Page Municipal Airport – PGA

Peach Springs, Grand Canyon West Airport – GCW

Phoenix Sky Harbor International Airport – PHX

Tucson International Airport – TUS

Yuma International Airport – YUM

Prescott Municipal Airport – PRC

Nevada

Boulder City Municipal Airport – BLD

Elko Regional Airport – EKO

Las Vegas, McCarran International Airport – LAS

Reno/Tahoe International Airport - RNO

New Mexico

Albuquerque International Sunport – ABQ

Hobbs, Lea County Regional Airport – HOB

Roswell International Air Center – ROW

Santa Fe Regional Airport – SAF

Farmington, Four Corners Regional Airport – FMN

Los Alamos Airport – LAM

Carlsbad, Cavern City Air Terminal – CNM

Clovis Municipal Airport – CVN

Silver City, Grant County Airport – SVC

Colorado

Aspen, Aspen-Pitkin County Airport – ASE

City of Colorado Springs Municipal Airport – COS

Denver International Airport – DEN

Durnago-La Plata County Airport – DRO

Eagle County Regional Airport – EGE

Grand Junction Regional Airport – GJT

Gunnison-Crested Butte Regional Airport – GUC

Hayden, Yampa Valley Airport – HDN

Montrose Regional Airport – MTJ

Alamosa, San Luis Valley Regional Airport – ALS

Cortez Municipal Airport – CEZ

Pueblo Memorial Airport – PUB

Telluride Regional Airport – TEX

Wyoming ■

Casper/Natrona County International Airport - CPR

Cody, Yellowstone Regional Airport – COD

Gillette-Campbell County Airport – GCC

Jackson, Jackson Hole Airport – JAC

Laramie Regional Airport – LAR

Rock Springs, Southwest Wyoming Regional Airport – RKS

Cheyenne Regional Airport – CYS

Riverton Regional Airport – RIW

Sheridan County Airport – SHR

North Dakota ◼️

Bismarck Municipal Airport — BIS

Dickinson, Theodore Roosevelt Regional Airport — DIK

Fargo, Hector International Airport — FAR

Grand Forks International Airport — GFK

Minot International Airport — MOT

Williston, Sloulin Field International Airport — ISN

Devils Lake Regional Airport — DVL

Jamestown Regional Airport — JMS

Minnesota ▮

Benidji Regional Airport — BJI

Brainerd Lakes Regional Airport — BRD

Duluth International Airport — DLH

Hibbing, Range Regional Airport — HIB

International Falls, Falls International Airport — INL

Minneapolis-St. Paul International Airport — MSP

Rochester International Airport — RST

St. Cloud Regional Airport — STC

Wisconsin

Appleton International Airport – ATW

Eau Claire, Chippewa Valley Regional Airport – EAU

Green Bay, Austin Straubel International Airport – GRB

La Crosse Regional Airport – LSE

Madison, Dane County Regional Airport – MSN

Milwaukee, Mitchell International Airport – MKE

Mosinee, Central Wisconsin Airport – CWA

Rhinelander, Oneida County Airport – RHI

Iowa

Cedar Rapids, The Eastern Iowa Airport – CID

Des Moines International Airport – DSM

Dubuque Regional Airport – DBQ

Sioux City, Sioux Gateway Airport – SUX

Waterloo Regional Airport – ALO

Burlington, Southeast Iowa Regional Airport – BRL

Fort Dodge Regional Airport – FOD

Mason City Municipal Airport – MCW

Missouri

Columbia Regional Airport – COU

Joplin Regional Airport – JLN

Kansas City International Airport – MCI

Springfield-Branson National Airport – SGF

St. Louis Lambert International Airport – STL

Branson Airport – BKG

Cape Girardeau Regional Airport – CGI

Fort Leonard Wood/Waynesville-St. Robert Regional Airport – TBN

Kirksville Regional Airport – IRK

Kansas

Garden City Regional Airport – GCK

Manhattan Regional Airport – MHK

Topeka Regional Airport – TOP

Wichita Dwight D. Eisenhower National Airport – ICT

Dodge City Regional Airport – DDC

Hays Regional Airport – HYS

Liberal Mid America Regional Airport – LBL

Salina Municipal Airport – SLN

Nebraska

Grand Island, Central Nebraska Regional Airport – GRI

Lincoln Airport – LNK

Omaha, Eppley Airfield – OMA

Kearney Regional Airport – EAR

North Platte Regional Airport – LBF

Scottsbluff, Western Nebraska Regional Airport – BFF

Alliance Municipal Airport – AIA

Chadron Municipal Airport – CDR

McCook Ben Nelson Regional Airport – MCK

South Dakota

Aberdeen Regional Airport – ABR

Rapid City Regional Airport – RAP

Sioux Falls Regional Airport – FSD

Pierre Regional Airport – PIR

Watertown Regional Airport – ATY

Texas 🖐

Abilene Regional Airport – ABI

Amarillo, Rick Husband Amarillo International Airport – AMA

Austin-Bergstrom International Airport – AUS

Beaumont/Port Arthur, Jack Brooks Regional Airport – BPT

Brownsville/South Padre Island International Airport – BRO

College Station, Easterwood Airport – CLL

Corpus Christi International Airport – CRP

Dallas 'Love Field' – DAL

Dallas/Fort Worth International Airport – DFW

El Paso International Airport – ELP

Killeen-Fort Hood Regional Airport – GRK

Harlingen, Valley International Airport – HRL

Houston, George Bush Intercontinental Airport – IAH

Laredo International Airport – LRD

Longview, East Texas Regional Airport – GGG

Lubbock Preston Smith International Airport – LBB

McAllen Miller International Airport – MFE

Midland International Airport – MAF

San Angelo Regional Airport – SJT

San Antonio International Airport – SAT

Tyler, Tyler Pounds Regional Airport – TYR

Waco Regional Airport – ACT

Wichita Falls Municipal Airport – SPS

Victoria Regional Airport – VCT

Louisiana

Alexandria International Airport – AEX

Baton Rouge Metropolitan Airport – BTR

Lafayette Regional Airport – LFT

Lake Charles Regional Airport – LCH

Monroe Regional Airport – MLU

(Louis Armstrong) New Orleans International Airport – MSY

Shreveport Regional Airport – SHV

Alabama

Birmingham-Shuttlesworth International Airport – BHM

Dothan Regional Airport – DHN

Huntsville International Airport – HSV

Mobile Regional Airport – MOB

Montgomery Regional Airport – MGM

Alaska

Ted Stevens Anchorage International Airport – ANC

Aniak Airport – ANI

Barrow, Wiley Post-Will Rogers Memorial Airport – BRW

Bethel Airport – BET

Cordova, Merle K. (Mudhole) Smith Airport – CDV

Deadhorse/Prudhoe Bay, Deadhorse Airport – SCC

Dillingham Airport – DLG

Fairbanks International Airport – FAI

Galena, Edward G. Pitka Sr. Airport – GAL

Homer Airport – HOM

Juneau International Airport – JNU

Kenai Municipal Airport – ENA

Ketchikan International Airport – KTN

King Salmon Airport – AKN

Kodiak Airport – ADQ

Kotzebue, Ralph Wien Memorial Airport – OTZ

Nome Airport – OME

Petersburg James A. Johnson Airport – PSG

Sitka Rocky Gutierrez Airport – SIT

St. Mary's Airport – KSM

Unalakleet Airport — UNK

Unalaska Airport — DUT

Valdez Airport — VDZ

Wrangell Airport — WRG

Yakutat Airport — YAK

Alakanuk Airport — AUK

Anaktuvuk Pass Airport - AKP

Atmautluak Airport — ATT

Buckland Airport — BKC

Chefornak Airport — CYF

Chevak Airport — VAK

Cold Bay Airport — CDB

Coldfoot Airport — CXF

Craig Seaplane Base — CGA

Eek Airport — EEK

Emmonak Airport — EMK

Fort Yukon Airport — FYU

Gambell Airport — GAM

Gustavus Airport — GST

Haines Airport — HNS

Hoonah Airport — HNH

Hooper Bay Airport — HPB

Huslia Airport — HSL

Iliamma Airport – ILI

Kaktovik/Barter Island, Barter Island LRRS Airport – BTI

Kalskag Airport – KLG

Kasigluk Airport – KUK

Kiana, Bob Baker Memorial Airport – IAN

Kipnuk Airport – KPN

Klawock Airport – KLW

Kongiganak Airport – KKH

Kotlik Airport – KOT

Kwethulk Airport – KWT

Kwigillingok Airport – KWK

Larsen Bay Airport – KLN

Manokotak Airport – KMO

Marshall Don Hunter Sr. Airport – MLL

McGrath Airport – MCG

Matlakatla Seaplane Base – MTM

Mountain Village Airport – MOU

Newtok Airport – WWT

Noatak Airport – WTK

Noorvik Airport – ORV

Nunapitchuk Airport – NUP

Old Harbor Airport – OLH

Pilot Station Airport – PQS

Point Hope Airport – PHO

Quinhagak Airport – KWN

Russian Mission Airport – RSH

St. Paul Island Airport – SNP

Sand Point Airport – SDP

Savoonga Airport – SVA

Scammon Bay Airport – SCM

Selawik Airport – WLK

Seldova Airport – SOV

Shishmaref Airport – SHH

Skagway Airport – SGY

Tanana, Ralph M. Calhoun Memorial Airport – TAL

Thorne Bay Seaplane Base – KTB

Toksook Bay Airport – OOK

Tuluksak Airport – TLT

Tuntutuliak Airport – WTL

Wainwright Airport - AIN

Arkansas

Fayetteville, Northwest Arkansas Regional Airport — XNA

Fort Smith Regional Airport — FSM

Little Rock, Bill & Hillary Clinton National Airport — LIT

Texarkana Regional Airport — TXK

El Dorado, South Arkansas Regional Airport — ELD

Harrison, Boone County Airport — HRO

Jonesboro Municipal Airport — JBR

Connecticut

Hartford, Bradley International Airport — BLD

New Haven, Tweed New Haven Regional Airport — HVN

Delaware

Wilmington Airport — ILG

Florida ⬦

Daytona Beach International Airport – DAB

Fort Lauderdale-Hollywood International Airport – FLL

Fort Myers, Southwest Florida International Airport – RSW

Gainesville Regional Airport – GNV

Jacksonville International Airport – JAX

Key West International – EYW

Melbourne, Orlando Melbourne International Airport – MLB

Miami International Airport – MIA

Panama City Beach, Northwest Florida Beaches International Airport – ECP

Pensacola International Airport – PNS

Punta Gorda Airport – PGD

Sarasota-Bradenton International Airport – SRQ

St. Augustine, Northeast Florida Regional Airport – UST

St. Petersburg/Clearwater, St. Pete-Clearwater International Airport – PIE

Tallahassee International Airport – TLH

Tampa International Airport – TPA

Valparaiso, Destin-Fort Walton Beach Airport – VPS

West Palm Beach, Palm Beach International Airport – PBI

Georgia ▶

Albany, Southwest Georgia Regional Airport — ABY

Hartfield-Jackson Atlanta International Airport — ATL

Augusta Regional Airport — AGS

Brunswick Golden Isles Airport — BQK

Columbus Metropolitan Airport — GSG

Savannah/Hilton Head International Airport — SAV

Valdosta Regional Airport — VLD

Athens Benn Epps Airport — AHN

Macon, Middle Georgia Regional Airport — MCN

Atlanta/Chamblee, DeKalb-Peachtree Airport — PDK

Hawaii ➘

Hilo International Airport — ITO

Honolulu, Daniel K. Inouye International Airport — HNL

Kahului Airport — OGG

Kailua-Kona, Kona International Airport at Keahole — KOA

Kaunakakai, Molokai Airport — MKK

Lanai Airport — LNY

Lihue Airport — LIH

Hana Airport — HNM

Kalaupapa Airport – LUP

Kamuela, Waimea-Kohala Airport – MUE

Lahaina, Kapalua Airport – JHM

Illinois 🔻

Belleville, MidAmerica St. Louis Airport – BLV

Bloomington/Normal, Central Illinois Regional Airport at Bloomington-Normal – BMI

Champaign/Urbana, University of Illinois-Willard Airport – CMI

Chicago O'Hare International Airport – ORD

Marion, Williamson County Regional Airport – MWA

Moline, Quad City International Airport – MLI

Peoria, General Wayne A. Downing Peoria International Airport – PIA

Quincy Regional Airport – UIN

Springfield, Abraham Lincoln Capital Airport – SPI

Decatur Airport – DEC

Indiana

Evansville Regional Airport – EVV

Fort Wayne International Airport – FWA

Indianapolis International Airport – IND

South Bend International Airport – SBN

Kentucky

Cincinnati/Covington, Cincinnati/Northern Kentucky International Airport – CVG

Lexington, Blue Grass Airport – LEX

Louisville International Airport – SDF

Owensboro-Daviess County Regional Airport – OWB

Paducah, Barkley Regional Airport – PAH

Maine

Bangor International Airport – BGR

Portland International Jetport – PWM

Presque Isle, Northern Maine Regional Airport at Presque Isle – PQI

Rockland, Knox County Regional Airport – RKD

Augusta State Airport – AUG

Bar Harbor, Hancock County-Bar Harbor Airport – BHB

Maryland

Baltimore/Glen Burnie, Baltimore/Washington International Thurgood Marshall Airport – BWI

Hagerstown Regional Airport – HGR

Salisbury, Salisbury-Ocean City Wicomico Regional Airport – SBY

Massachusetts

Boston, Gen. Edward Lawrence Logan International Airport – BOS

Hyannis, Barnstable Municipal Airport – HYA

Nantucket Memorial Airport – ACK

Provincetown Municipal Airport – PVC

Vineyard Haven, Martha's Vineyard Airport – MVY

Worcester Regional Airport – ORH

New Bedford Regional Airport – EWB

Michigan 🦫

Alpena County Regional Airport – APN

Detroit/Romulus, Detroit Metropolitan Wayne County Airport – DTW

Escanaba, Delta County Airport – ESC

Flint, Bishop International Airport – FNT

Grand Rapids, Gerald R. Ford International Airport – GRR

Hancock/Calumet, Houghton County Memorial Airport – CMX

Iron Mountain/Kingsford, Ford Airport – IMT

Kalamazoo/Battle Creek International Airport – AZO

Lansing, Capital Region International Airport – LAN

Marquette/Gwinn, Sawyer International Airport – MQT

Muskegon County Airport – MKG

Pellston Regional Airport of Emmet County – PLN

Saginaw, MBS International Airport – MBS

Sault Ste. Marie, Chippewa County International Airport – CIU

Traverse City, Cherry Capital Airport – TVC

Charlevoix Municipal Airport – CVX

Ironwood, Gogebic-Iron County Airport – IWD

Mississippi

Columbus/West Point/Starkville, Golden Triangle Regional Airport – GTR

Gulfport-Biloxi International Airport – GPT

Jackson, Jackson-Evers International Airport – JAN

Greenville, Mid Delta Regional Airport – GLH

Hattiesburg-Laurel Regional Airport – PIB

Meridian Regional Airport – MEI

Tunica Municipal Airport – UTM

Tupelo Regional Airport – TUP

North Carolina

Asheville Regional Airport – AVL

Charlotte/Douglas International Airport – CLT

Concord Regional Airport – USA

Fayetteville Regional Airport – FAY

Greensboro, Piedmont Triad International Airport – GSO

Greenville, Pitt-Greenville Airport – PGV

Jacksonville, Albert J. Ellis Airport – OAJ

New Bern, Coastal Carolina Regional Airport – EWN

Raleigh-Durham International Airport – RDU

Wilmington International Airport – ILM

Kinston Regional Jetport at Stallings Field – ISO

New Hampshire ▲

Lebanon Municipal Airport – LEB

Manchester-Boston Regional Airport – MHT

Portsmouth International Airport – PSM

New Jersey ▮

Atlantic City International Airport – ACY

Trenton Mercer Airport – TTN

Newark Liberty International Airport – EWR

Morristown Municipal Airport – MMU

New York ◀

Albany International Airport – ALB

Binghamton, Greater Binghamton Airport – BGM

Buffalo Niagara International Airport – BUF

Elmira/Corning Regional Airport – ELM

Farmingdale, Republic Airport – FRG

Islip, Long Island MacArthur Airport – ISP

Ithaca Thompkins Regional Airport – ITH

New York, John F. Kennedy International Airport – JFK

New York, LaGuardia Airport – LGA

Newburgh, Stewart International Airport – SWF

Niagara Falls International Airport – IAG

Plattsburgh International Airport – PBG

Rochester, Greater Rochester International Airport – ROC

Syracuse Hancock International Airport – SYR

Watertown International Airport – ART

White Plaines, Westchester County Airport – HPN

Jamestown, Chautauqua County/Jamestown Airport – JHW

Massena International Airport – MSS

Ogdensburg International Airport – OGS

Saranac Lake, Adirondack Regional Airport – SLK

Ohio

Akron-Canton Regional Airport – CAK

Cincinnati Municipal Lunken Airport – LUK

Cleveland, Hopkins International Airport – CLE

Columbus, John Glenn Columbus International Airport – LCK

Dayton, James M. Cox Dayton International Airport – DAY

Toledo Express Airport – TOL

Youngstown/Warren Regional Airport – YNG

Oklahoma

Lawton, Fort Sill Regional Airport – LAW

Oklahoma City, Will Rogers World Airport – OKC

Tulsa International Airport – TUL

Stillwater Regional Airport – SWO

Pennsylvania 🖤

Allentown, Lehigh Valley International Airport — ABE

Erie International Airport — ERI

Harrisburg/Middletown, Harrisburg International Airport — MDT

Latrobe, Arnold Palmer Regional Airport — LBE

Philadelphia International Airport — PHL

Pittsburgh International Airport — PIT

State College, University Park Airport — SCE

Wilkes-Barre/Scranton International Airport — AVP

Williamsport Regional Airport — IPT

Altoona, Altoona-Blair County Airport — AOO

DuBois/Falls Creek, DuBois Regional Airport — DUJ

Johnstown, John Murtha Johnstown-Cambria County Airport — JST

Lancaster Airport — LNS

Bradford Regional Airport — BFD

Franklin, Venango Regional Airport — FKL

Rhode Island

Brock Island/New Shoreham, Brock Island State Airport – BID

Providence/Warwick, Theodore Francis Green State Airport – PVD

Westerly State Airport – WST

South Carolina ♥

Charleston International Airport – CHS

Columbia Metropolitan Airport – CAE

Florence Regional Airport – FLO

Greenville, Greenville-Spartanburg International Airport – GSP

Hilton Head Island, Hilton Head Airport – HHH

Myrtle Beach International Airport – MYR

Tennessee

Bristol/Johnson City/Kingsport, Tri-Cities Regional Airport – TRI

Chattanooga Metropolitan Airport – CHA

Knoxville, McGhee Tyson Airport – TYS

Memphis International Airport – MEM

Nashville International Airport – BNA

Vermont

Burlington International Airport – BTV

Rutland, Southern Vermont Regional Airport – RUT

Virginia

Charlottesville-Ablemarle Airport – CHO

Lynchburg Regional Airport – LYH

Newport News/Williamsburg International Airport – PHF

Norfolk International Airport – ORF

Richmond International Airport – RIC

Roanoke Regional Airport – ROA

Washington D.C./Dulles/Chantilly, Washington Dulles International Airport – IAD

Staunton/Waynesboro/Harrisonburg, Shenandoah Valley
Regional Airport – SHD

West Virginia

Bridgeport, North Central West Virginia Airport – CKB

Charleston, Yeager Airport – CRW

Huntington, Tri-State Airport – HTS

Morgantown Municipal Airport – MGW

Beckley, Raleigh County Memorial Airport – BKW

Lewisburg, Breenbrier Valley Airport – LWB

Parkersburg, Mid-Ohio Valley Regional Airport – PKB

CANADA

British Columbia

Abbotsford International Airport — YXX

Anahim Lake Airport — YAA

Bella Coola Airport — QBC

Campbell River Airport — YBL

Castlegar, West Kootenay Regional Airport — YCG

Chilliwack Municipal Airport — YCW

Comox Valley Airport — YQQ

Cranbrook, Canadian Rockies International Airport — YXC

Dawson Creek Regional Airport — YDQ

Fort Nelson, Northern Rockies Regional Airport — YYE

Fort St. John, North Peace Regional Airport — YXJ

Kamloops Airport — YKA

Kelowna International Airport — YLW

Masset Municipal Airport — ZMT

Nanaimo Airport — YCD

Penticton Regional Airport — YYF

Pitt Meadows Regional Airport - YPK

Prince George Airport — YXS

Prince Rupert Airport — YPR

Quesnel Regional Airport — YQZ

Sandspit Airport – YZP

Smithers Regional Airport – YYD

Terrace-Kitimat, Northwest Regional Airport – YXT

Tofino-Long Beach Airport – YAZ

Vancouver International Airport – YVR

Vernon Regional Airport - YVK

Victoria International Airport – YYJ

Williams Lake Regional Airport - YWL

Alberta

Calgary International Airport – YYC

Edmonton International Airport – YEG

Edson Airport – YET

Fort Chipewyan Airport – YPY

Fort McMurray Airport – YMM

Grande Prairie Airport – YQU

High Level Airport – YOJ

Lethbridge County Airport – YQL

Lloydminster Airport – YLL

Medicine Hat Regional Airport – YXH

Peace River Airport – YPE

Rainbow Lake Airport – YOP

Red Deer Regional Airport – YQF

Rocky Mountain House Airport – YRM

Slave Lake Airport – YZH

Wainwright Aerodrome – YWV

Whitecourt Airport - YZU

Saskatchewan

Buffalo Narrows Airport – YVT

Estevan Regional Aerodrome – YEN

Fond-du-Lac Airport – ZFD

Hudson Bay Airport – YHB

Key Lake Airport - YKJ

Kindersley Regional Airport – YKY

La Ronge, Barber Field Airport – YVC

Meadow Lake Airport – YLJ

Moose Jaw Municipal Airport – YMJ

Nipawin Airport – YBU

North Battleford Airport – YQW

Points North Landing Airport – YNL

Prince Albert, Glass Field Airport - YPA

Regina International Airport – YQR

Saskatoon, John G Diefenbaker International Airport – YXE

Stoney Rapids Airport – YSF

Swift Current Airport – YYN

Tisdale Airport – YTT

Uranium City Airport – YBE

Wollaston Lake Airport – ZWL

Yorkton Municipal Airport – YQV

Manitoba

Berens River Airport — YBV

Bloodvein River Airport - YDV

Brandon Municipal Airport — YBR

Brochet Airport — YBT

Churchill Airport — YYQ

Cross Lake, Charlie Sinclair Memorial Airport — YCR

Flin Flon Airport — YFO

Gillam Airport — YGX

Gimli Industrial Park Airport — YGM

Gods Lake Narrows Airport — YGO

Gods River Airport — ZGI

Ilford Airport - ILF

Island Lake Airport — YIV

Kelsey Airport — KES

Lac Brochet Airport — XLB

Leaf Rapids Airport — YLR

Little Grand Rapids Airport - ZGR

Lynn Lake Airport — YYL

Norway House Airport - YNE

Oxford House Airport — YOH

Pikwitonei Airport — PIW

Poplar River Airport — XPP

Portage la Prairie/Southport Airport — YPG

Pukatawagan Airport — XPK

Red Sucker Lake Airport — YRS

St. Theresa Point Airport — YST

Shamattawa Airport — ZTM

South Indian Lake Airport — XSI

Swan River Airport — ZJN

Tadoule Lake Airport — XTL

The Pas Airport — YQD

Thicket Portage Airport — YTD

Thompson Airport — YTH

Winnipeg, James Armstrong Richardson International Airport — YWG

York Factory, York Landing Airport — ZAC

Ontario

Armstrong Airport – YYW

Atikokan Municipal Airport – YIB

Attawapiskat Airport – YAT

Bearskin Lake Airport – XBE

Brantford Airport – YFD

Brockville Regional Tackaberry Airport – XBR

Centralia, James T. Field Memorial Aerodrome – YCE

Chapleau Airport – YLD

Chatham-Kent Airport – XCM

Cochrane Aerodrome – YCN

Cornwall Regional Airport – YCC
Dryden Regional Airport – YHD

Eabametoong, Fort Hope Airport

Earlton, Timiskaming Regional Airport

Elliot Lake Municipal Airport, YEL

Fort Albany Airport – YFA

Fort Frances Municipal Airport – YAG

Fort Severn Airport – YER

Geraldton, Greenstone Regional Airport – YGQ

Goderich Airport – YGD

Gore Bay, Manitoulin Airport – YZE

Greater Sudbury Airport — YSB

Hamilton, John C. Munro Hamilton International Airport — YHM

Hearst, René Fontaine Municipal Airport — YHF

Hornepayne Municipal Airport — YHN

Ignace Municipal Airport — ZUC

Kapuskasing Airport — YYU

Kasabonika Airport — XKS

Kashechewan Airport — ZKE

Keewayin Airport — KEW

Kenora Airport — YQK

Kincardine Airport — YKD

Kingfisher Lake Airport — KIF

Kingston, Norman Rogers Airport — YGK

Kirkland Lake Airport — YKX

Kitchenuhmaykoosib Inninuwug, Big Trout Lake Airport — YTL

London International Airport — YXU

Manitouwadge Airport — YMG

Manitouwaning/Manitoulin East Municipal Airport — YEM

Marathon Aerodrome — YSP

Marten Falls, Ogoki Post Airport — YOG

Midland/Huronia Airport — YEE

Moosonee Airport — YMO

Muskoka Airport — YQA

Muskrat Dam Airport — MSA
Nakina Airport — YQN

Neskantaga, Lansdowne House Airport — YLH

Nibinamik, Summer Beaver Airport — SUR

North Bay/Jack Garland Airport — YYB

North Spirit Lake Airport — YNO

Ottawa, Macdonald Cartier International Airport — YOW

Owen Sound, Billy Bishop Regional Airport — YOS

Parry Sound Area Municipal Airport — YPD

Peawanuck Airport — YPO

Pembroke Airport — YTA

Peterborough Airport — YPQ

Pickle Lake Airport — YPL

Pikangikum Airport — YPM

Poplar Hill Airport — YHP

Red Lake Airport — YRL

Kitchener/Waterloo, Region of Waterloo International
Airport — YKF

Sachigo Lake Airport — ZPB

St. Catharines/Niagara District Airport — YCM

St. Thomas Municipal Airport — YQS

Sandy Lake Airport – ZSJ

Sarina, Chris Hadfield Airport – YZR

Sault Ste. Marie Airport – YAM

Sioux Lookout Airport – YXL

Smiths Falls-Montague Airport – YSH

Thunder Bay International Airport – YQT

Timmins/Victor M. Power Airport – YTS

Toronto, Pearson International Airport – YYZ

Trenton Airport – YTR

Wapekeka, Angling Lake/Wapekeka Airport – YAX

Wawa Airport – YXZ

Webequie Airport – YWP

White River Water Aerodrome – YWR

Wiarton Airport – YVV
Windsor Airport – YQG

Wunnumin Lake Airport – WNN

Quebec

Akulivik Airport – AKV

Alma Airport – YTF

Amos/Magny Airport – YEY

Aupaluk Airport – YPJ

Bagotville Airport – YBG

Baie-Comeau Airport – YBC

Blanc-Sablon, Lourdes-de-Blanc-Sablon Airport – YBX

Bonaventure Airport – YVB

Bromont, Roland Désourdy Airport – ZBM

Charlevoix Airport – YML

Chevery Airport – YHR

Chibougamau/Chapais Airport – YMT

Chiasibi Airport – YKU

Dolbeau-Mistassini, Dolbeau-Saint-Félicien Airport – YDO

Eastmain River Airport – ZEM

Forestville Airport – YFE

Gaspé, Michel-Pouilot Airport – YGP

Gatineau-Ottawa Executive Airport – YND

Havre Saint-Pierre Airport – YGV

Inukjuak Airport – YPH

Ivujivik Airport – YIK

Kangiqsualujjuaq, Georges River Airport – XGR

Kangirsuk Airport – YKG

Kattiniq/Donaldson Airport – YAU

Kuujjuaq Airport – YVP

Kuujjuarapik Airport – YGW

La Romaine Airport – ZGS

La Sarre Airport – SSQ

La Tabatière Airport – ZLT

La Turque Airport – YLQ

Lebel-sur-Quévillon Airport – YLS

Magdalen Islands, Îles-de-la-Madeleine Airport – YGR

Maniwaki Airport – YMW

Matagami Airport – YNM

Matane Airport – YME

Mont-Joli Airport – YYY

Montreal, Pierre Elliott Trudeau International Airport – YUL

Natashquan Airport – YNA

Nemaska, Nemiscau Airport – YNS

Passes-Dangereuses, Chutes-des-Passes/Lac Margane Water Aerodrome – YWQ

Port-Menier Airport – YPN

Quaqtaq Airport – YQC

Quebec City, Jean Lesage International Airport – YQB

Radisson, La Grande Rivière Airport – YGL

Rimouski Airport – YXK

Riviere-du-Loup Airport – YRI

Roberval Airport – YRJ

Rouyn-Noranda Airport – YUY

Saint Augustin Airport – YIF

Saint-Jean-sur-Richelieu, Saint-Jean Airport – YJN

Salluit Airport – YZG

Schefferville Airport – YKL

Sept-Îles Airport – YZV

Sherbrooke Airport – YSC

Tasiujaq Airport – YTQ

Tête-à-La-Baleine Airport – ZTB

Trois-Rivières Airport – YRQ

Umiujaq Airport – YUD

Val-d'Or Airport – YVO

Waskaganish Airport – YKQ

Wemindji Airport – YNC

New Brunswick

Bathurst Airport – ZBF

Charlo Airport – YCL

Fredericton International Airport – YFC

Miramichi Airport – YCH

Moncton, Greater Moncton Roméo LeBlanc International Airport – YQM

Saint John Airport – YSJ

Saint Léonard Aerodrome – YSL

Prince Edward Island

Charlottetown Airport – YYG

Summerside Airport – YSU

Nova Scotia

Digby/Annapolis Regional Airport – YDG

Fox Harbour Airport – YFX

Greenwood Airport – YZX

Halifax Stanfield International Airport – YHZ

Port Hawkesbury Airport – YPS

Sydney, J.A. Douglas McCurdy Airport – YQY

Yarmouth Airport – YQI

Newfoundland & Labrador

Black Tickle Airport – YBI

Cartwright Airport – YRF

Charlottetown Airport – YHG

Churchill Falls Airport – ZUM

Deer Lake Regional Airport – YDF
Gander International Airport – YQX

Happy Valley Goose Bay, Goose Bay Airport – YYR

Hopedale Airport – YHO

Makkovik Airport – YMN

Mary's Harbour Airport – YMH

Nain Airport – YDP

Port Hope Simpson Airport – YHA

Postville Airport – YSO

Rigolet Airport – YRG

St. Anthony Airport – YAY

St. John's International Airport – YYT

Stephenville International Airport – YJT

Wabush Airport – YWK

Yukon

Beaver Creek Airport – YXQ

Burwash Airport – YDB

Dawson City Airport – YDA
Faro Airport – ZFA

Haines Junction Airport – YHT

Mayo Airport – YMA

Old Crow Airport – YOC

Ross River Airport – YDM

Teslin Airport – YZW

Watson Lake Airport – YQH

Whitehorse, Erik Nielsen Whitehorse International Airport – YXY

Northwest Territories

Aklavik, Freddie Carmichael Airport – LAK

Colville Lake, Tommy Kochon Aerodrome – YCK

Déline Airport – YWJ

Fort Good Hope Airport – YGH

Fort Liard Airport – YJF

Fort McPherson Airport – ZFM

Fort Resolution Airport – YFR

Fort Simpson Airport – YFS

Fort Smith Airport – YSM

Gamèti/Rae Lakes Airport – YRA

Great Bear Lake Airport – DAS

Hay River, Merlyn Carter Airport – YHY

Inuvik, Mike Zubko Airport – YEV

Norman Wells Airport – YVQ

Paulatuk, Nora Aliqatchialuk Ruben Airport – YPC

Sachs Harbour, David Nasogaluak Jr. Saaryuaq Airport – YSY

Tuktoyaktuk, James Gruben Airport – YUB

Tulita Airport – ZFN

Ulukhaktok/Holman Airport – YHI

Wrigley Airport – YWY

Yellowknife Airport – YZF

Nunavut

Alert Airport – YLT

Arctic Bay Airport - YAB

Arviat Airport – YEK

Baker Lake Airport – YBK

Cambridge Bay Airport – YCB

Cape Dorset Airport – YTE

Chesterfield Inlet Airport – YCS

Clyde River – YCY

Coral Harbour Airport – YZS

Doris Lake Aerodrome – JOJ

Eureka Aerodrome – YEU

Gjoa Haven Airport – YHK

Grise Ford Airport – YGZ

Hall Beach Airport – YUX

Hope Bay Aerodrome – UZM

Igloolik Airport – YGT

Iqaluit Airport – YFB

Kimmirut Airport – YLC
Kugaaruk Airport – YBB

Kugluktuk Airport – YCO

Mary River Aerodrome – YMV

Naujaat Airport – YUT

Pangnirtung Airport – YXP

Pond Inlet Airport – YIO

Qikiqtarjuaq Airport – YVM

Rankin Inlet Airport – YRT

Resolute Bay Airport – YRB

Sanikiluaq Airport – YSK

Taloyoak Airport – YYH

Tanquary Fjord Airport – JQ6

Whale Cove Airport - YXN

ANTIGUA & BARBUDA

St John's, V.C. Bird International Airport – ANU

Codrington, Barbuda Codrington Airport – BBQ

BAHAMAS

Marsh Harbour Airport – MHH

Treasure Cay Airport – TCB

Andros Town Airport – ASD

Nicholls Town – San Andros Airport – SAQ

Bimini, South Bimini Airport – BIM

Arthur's Town Airport – ATC

New Bright Airport – TBI

Colonel Hill Airport – CRI

Governor's Harbour Airport – GHB

North Eleuthera Airport – ELH

Rock Sound International Airport – RSD

Great Exuma Island, Exuma International Airport – GGT

Grand Bahama International Airport – FPO

Matthew Town, Inagua Airport – IGA

Mayaguana Airport – MYG

Nassau, Lynden Pindling International Airport – NAS

San Salvador Airport – ZSA

BARBADOS

Bridgetown, Grantley Adams International Airport – BGI

BELIZE

Belize City, Philip S. W. Goldson International Airport – BZE

Belmopan, Hector Silva Airstrip – BCV

Big Creek Airstrip – BGK

Caye Caulker Airport – CUK

Caye Chapel Airport – CYC

Corozal Airport – CZH

Dangriga Airport – DGA

Hope Creek, Melinda Airport – MDB

Independence Airport – INB

Orange Walk Airstrip – ORZ

Placencia Airport – PLJ

Punta Gorda Airport – PND

San Ignacio, Matthew Spain Airport – SQS

San Pedro, John Grief II Airport – SPR

Sarteneja Airstrip – SJX

Silver Creek Airport – SVK

Spanish Lookout, Manatee Airport – MZE

COSTA RICA

Liberia, Daniel Oduber Quirós International Airport – LIR

Limón International Airport – LIO

San José, Tobías Bolaños International Airport – SYQ

CUBA

Baracoa, Gustavo Rizo Airport – BCA

Bayamo, Carlos Manuel de Céspedes Airport – BYM

Camagüey, Ignacio Argamonte International Airport – CMW

Cayo Coco, Jardines del Rey Airport – CCC

Cayo Largo del Sur, Vili Acuña Airport – CYO

Cienfuegos, Jaime González Airport – CFG

Guantánamo, Mariana Grajales Airport – GAO

Havana, José Martí International Airport – HAV

Holguín, Frank País Airport – HOG

Las Tunas, Hermanos Ameijeiras Airport – VTU

Manzanillo, Sierra Maestra Airport – MZO

Moa, Orestes Acosta Airport – MOA

Nueva Gerona, Rafael Cabrera Airport – GER

Santa Clara, Abel Santamaría Airport – SNU

Santiago de Cuba, Antonio Maceo Airport – SCU

Varadero, Juan Gualberto Gómez Airport – VRA

DOMINICA

Marigot, Douglas-Charles Airport – DOM

Roseau, Canefield Airport – DCF

DOMINICAN REPUBLIC

Barahona, María Montez International Airport – BRX

La Romana International Airport – LRM

Puerto Plata, Gregorio Luperón International Airport – POP

Punta Cana/Higüey, Punta Cana International Airport – PUJ

Sánchez, Samaná El Catey International Airport – AZS

Santiago de los Caballeros, Cibao International Airport – STI

Santo Domingo, Las Américas-JFPG International Airport – SDQ

EL SALVADOR

San Salvador, Óscar Arnulfo Romero International Airport – SAL

GRENADA

St. George's, Maurice Bishop International Airport – GND

Hillsborough, Lauriston Airport – CRU

GUATEMALA

Flores, Mundo Maya International Airport – FRS

Guatemala City, La Aurora International Airport – GUA

Puerto Barrios Airport – PBR

HAITI

Cap-Haïtien International Airport – CAP

Port-au-Prince, Toussaint Louverture International Airport – PAP

HONDURAS

Guanaja Airport – GJA

La Ceiba, Golosón International Airport – LCE

Puerto Lempira Airport – PEU

Roatán, Juan Manuel Gálvez International Airport – RTB

San Pedro Sula, Ramón Villeda Morales International Airport – SAP

Tegucigalpa, Toncontín International Airport – TGU

Útila Airport – UII

JAMAICA

Kingston, Norman Manley International Airport — KIN

Montego Bay, Sangster International Airport — MBJ

Ocho Rios/Boscobel, Ian Fleming International Airport — OCJ

Negril Aerodrome — NEG

Port Antonio — POT

MEXICO

Acapulco, General Juan N. Álvarez International Airport — ACA

Aguascalientes, Lic. Jesús Terán Pedro International Airport — AGU

Campeche, Ing. Alberto Acuña Ongay International Airport — CPE

Cancún International Airport — CUN

Chetumal International Airport — CTM

Chichen Itza International Airport — CZA

Chihuahua, General Roberto Fierro Villalobos International Airport — CUU

Ciudad Acuña International Airport — ACN

Ciudad Constitución Airport — CUA

Ciudad del Carmen International Airport — CME

Ciudad Mante National Airport – MMC

Ciudad Juárez, Abraham González International Airport – CJS

Ciudad Obregón International Airport – CEN

Ciudad Victoria, General Pedro J. Méndez International Airport – CVM

Colima, Lic. Miguel de la Madrid Airport – CLQ

Cozumel International Airport - CZM

Cuernavaca, General Mariano Matamoros Airport – CVJ

Cuilacán, Federal de Bachigualto International Airport – CUL

Durango, General Guadelupe Victoria International Airport – DGO

Guadalajara, Don Miguel Hidalgo y Costilla International Airport – DGL

Guasave, Campo Cuatro Milpas Airport – GSV

Guaymas, General José María Yáñez International Airport – GYM

Guerrero Negro Airport – GUB

Hermosillo, General Ignacio Pesqueria Garcia International Airport – HMO

Huatulco – Bahías de Huatulco International Airport – HUX

Isla Mejeres National Airport – ISJ

Ixtapa-Zihuantanejo International Airport – ZIH

La Paz, Manuel Márquez de León International Airport – LAP

Lázaro Cárdenas Airport – LZC

León, Del Bajío International Airport – BJX

Loreto International Airport – LTO

Los Cabos International Airport – SJD

Los Mochis, Federal del Valle del Fuerte International Airport – LMM

Manzanillo, Playa de Oro International Airport – ZLO

Matamoros, General Servando Canales International Airport – MAM

Mazatlán, General Rafael Buelna International Airport – MZT

Mérida, Manuel Crescencio Rejón International Airport – MID

Mexicali, General Rodolfo Sánchez Taboada International Airport – MXL

Mexico City, Aeropuerto Internacional Benito Juárez – MEX

Minatitlán/Coatzacoalcos National Airport – MTT

Monclova, Venustiano Carranza International Airport – LOV

Monterrey, Del Norte International Airport – NTR

Morelia, General Francisco J. Mujica International Airport – MLM

Nogales International Airport – NOG

Nuevo Casas Grandes Municipal Airport – NCG

Nuevo Laredo, Quetzalcóatl International Airport – NLD

Oaxaca, Xoxocotlán International Airport – OAX

Palenque International Airport – PQM

Piedras Negras International Airport – PDS

Poza Rica, El Tajín National Airport – PAZ

Puebla, Hermanos Sardán International Airport – PBC

Puerto Escondido International Airport – PXM

Puerto Peñasco International Airport – PPE

Puerto Vallarta, Lic. Gustavo Diaz Ordaz International Airport – PVR

Reynosa, General Lucio Blanco International Airport – REX

Saltillo, Plan de Guadalupe International Airport – SLW

San Felipe International Airport – SFH

San Luis Potosí, Ponciano Arriga International Airport – SLP

Tampico, General Francisco Javier Mina International Airport – TAM

Tamuín National Airport – TSL

Tapachula International Airport – TAP

Tehuacàn National Airport – TCN

Tepic, Amado Nervo National Airport – TPQ

Tijuana, General Abelardo L. Rodríguez International Airport – TIJ

Tizimín, Cupul National Airport – TLC

Torreón, Francisco Sarabia International Airport – TRC

Uruapan International Airport – UPN

Veracruz, General Heriberto Jara International Airport – VER

Villahermosa, Carlos Rovirosa Pérez International Airport – VSA

Xalapa, El Lancero Airport – JAL

Zacatecas, General Leobardo C. Ruiz. International Airport – ZCL

NICARAGUA

Managua, Augusto C. Sandino International Airport – MGA

Bilwi, Puerto Cabezas Airport – PUZ

Bluefields Airport – BEF

Corn Island Airport – RNI

San Carlos Airport – NCR

Tola, Costa Esmeralda Airport – ECI

PANAMA

Achutupo Airport – ACU

Arraiján, Panamá Pacifico International Airport – AIL

Bocas del Toro, Isla Colón International Airport – BOC

Changuinola, Capitán Manuel Niño International Airport – CHX

Chitré Alonso Valderrama Airport – CTD

Colón, Enrique Adolfo Jiménez Airport – ONX

Contadora Island, Contadora Airport – OTD

Corazón de Jesús Airport – CZJ

David, Enrique Malek International Airport - DAV

El Porvenir Airport – PVE

El Real Airport – ELE

Garachiné Airport – GHE

Jaqué Airport – JQE

Mulatupo Airport – MPP

Panama City, Tocumen International Airport – PTY

Pedasí, Capt. J. Montenegro Airport – PDM

Playón Chico Airport – PYC

Puerto Obaldia Airport – PUE

Puerto Piña, Bahía Piña Airport – BFQ

Rio Hato, Scarlett Martínez International Airport – RIH

Sambú Airport – SAX

Santiago, Ruben Cantu Airport – SYP

SAINT KITTS & NEVIS

Basseterre, Robert L. Bradshaw International Airport – SKB

Charlestown, Vance W. Armory International Airport – NEV

SAINT LUCIA

Castries, George F. L. Charles Airport – SLU

Vieux-Fort, Hewanorra International Airport – UVF

SAINT VINCENT AND THE GRENADINES

Argyle International Airport – SVD

Bequia, J. F. Mitchell Airport – BQU

Canouan Airport – CIW

Union Island Airport – UNI

TRINIDAD & TOBAGO

Port of Spain/Piarco, Piarco International Airport – POS

Scarborough/Crown Point – A.N.R. Robinson
International Airport – TAB

North American Dependant Territories

ANGUILLA (UK)

The Valley, Clayton J. Lloyd International Airport — AXA

ARUBA (NETHERLANDS)

Oranjestad, Queen Beatrix International Airport — AUA

BERMUDA (UK)

St. George's, L.F. Wade International Airport — BDA

BONAIRE (NETHERLANDS)

Kralendijk, Flamingo International Airport — BON

BRITISH VIRGIN ISLANDS (UK)

Beef Island/Tortola, Terrance B. Lettsome International Airport — EIS

Virgin Gorda Airport — VIJ

CAYMAN ISLANDS (UK)

George Town/Grand Cayman, Owen Roberts International Airport – GCM

Cayman Brac, Charles Kirkconnell International Airport – CYB

Little Cayman, Edward Bodden Airfield – LYB

CURAÇAO (NETHERLANDS)

Willemstad, Hato International Airport – CUR

GREENLAND (DENMARK)

Aasiaat Airport - JEG

Ilulissat Airport – JAV

Ittoqqortoormiit, Nerlerit Inaat Airport – CNP

Kangerlussuaq Airport – SFJ

Kulusuk Airport – KUS

Maniitsoq Airport – JSU

Narsarsuaq Airport – UAK

Nuuk Airport – GOH

Paamiut Airport – JFR

Qaanaaq Airport – NAQ

Qaarsut/Uummannaq, Qaarsut Airport – JQA

Sisimiut Airport – JHS

Upernavik Airport – JUV

GUADELOUPE (FRANCE)

Grand-Bourg, Marie Galante Airport – GBJ

Pointe-à-Pitre Airport – PTP

Saint-François Airport – SFC

MARTINIQUE (FRANCE)

Fort-de-France/Lamentin, Martinique Aimé Césaire International Airport – FDF

MONTSERRAT (UK)

Gerald's, John A Osborne Airport – MNI

PUERTO RICO

Aguadilla, Rafael Hernández International Airport – BQN

Ceiba, José Aponte de la Torre Airport – NRR

Culebra, Benjamín Rivera Noriega Airport – CPX

Ponce, Mercedita International Airport – PSE

San Juan/Carolina, Luis Muños Marín International Airport – SJU

Vieques, Antonio Rivera Rodríquez Airport – VQS

Mayagüez, Eugenio María de Hostos Airport – MAZ

SABA (NETHERLANDS)

Saba, Juancho E. Yrausquin Airport – SAB

SAINT BARTHELEMY (FRANCE)

St. Jean/Saint Barthélemy, Gustaf III Airport – SBH

SAINT MARTIN (FRANCE)

Grand Case, L'Espérance Airport – SFG

SINT MAARTEN (NETHERLANDS)

Philipsburg, Princess Juliana International Airport – SXM

SAINT PIERRE & MIQUELON

Saint-Pierre Airport – FSP

Miquelon Airport – MQC

SINT EUSTATIUS (NETHERLANDS)

Sint Eusatius, F.D. Roosevelt Airport – EUX

TURKS & CAICOS ISLANDS (UK)

Grand Turk Island, JAGS McCartney International Airport – GDT

North Caicos Airport – NCA

Providenciales International Airport – PLS

Salt Cay Airport – SLX

South Caicos Airport – XSC

US VIRGIN ISLANDS (US)

Charlotte Amalie/St. Thomas, Cyril E. King Airport – STT

Christiansted/St. Croix, Henry E. Rohlsen Airport - STX

Airport Codes

of

Europe &

Oceania

ALBANIA

Tirana International Airport – TIA

ARMENIA

Gyumri, Shirak International Airport – LWN

Yerevan, Zvartnots International Airport – EVN

AUSTRIA

Graz Airport – GRZ

Innsbruck Airport – INN

Klagenfurt Airport – KLU

Linz Airport – LNZ

Salzburg Airport – SZG

Vienna International Airport – VIE

AZERBAIJAN

Baku, Heydar Aliyev International Airport – GYD

Ganja International Airport – KVD

Lankaran International Airport – LLK

Nakchivan Interntional Airport – NAJ

Qabala International Airport – GBB

Zaqatala International Airport - ZTU

BELARUS

Brest Airport – BQT

Homiel, Gomel Airport – GME

Hronda Airport – GNA

Minsk National Airport – MSQ

BELGIUM

Antwerp International Airport – ANR

Bruges/Ostend International Airport – OST

Brussels/Zaventem, Brussels Airport – BRU

Charleroi, Brussels South Charleroi Airport – CRL

Kortrijk/Wevelgem, Flanders International Airport – KJK

Liège Airport – LGG

BOSNIA & HERZEGOVINA

Banja Luka International Airport – BNX

Mostar International Airport – OMO

Sarajevo International Airport – SJJ

Tuzla International Airport – TZL

BULGARIA

Burgas/Sarafovo, Burgas Airport – BOJ

Plovdiv/Krumovo, Plovdiv Airport – PDV

Sofia Airport – SOF

Varna/Aksakovo, Varna Airport – VAR

CROATIA

Brac Airport – BWK

Dubrovnik Airport – DBV

Mali Lošinj, Lošinj Airport – LSZ

Osijek Airport – OSI

Pula Airport – PUY

Rijeka Airport – RJK

Split Airport – SPU

Zadar Airport – ZAD

Zagreb, Franjo Tudman Airport – ZAG

CYPRUS

Larnaca International Airport – LCA

Paphos International Airport – PFO

Nicosia International Airport – NIC

Tymvou, Ercan International Airport – ECN

CZECHIA

Prague, Václav Havel Airport – PRG

Brno, Brno-Turany Airport – BRQ

Ostrava Airport – OSR

Karlovy Vary Airport – KLV

Pardubice Airport – PED

DENMARK

Aalborg/Nørresundby, Aalborg Airport – AAL

Aarhus Airport – AAR

Billund Airport – BLL

Bornholm/Rønne, Bornholm Airport – RNN

Copenhagen Airport, Kastrup – CPH

Esbjerg Airport – EBJ

Karup/Herning, Karup Airport – KRP

Læsø Airport – BYR

Odense, Hans Christian Anderson Airport – ODE

Sønderborg Airport – SGD

ESTONIA

Kuressaare Airport – URE

Kärdla/Hiiessaare, Kärdla Airport – KDL

Pärnu/Eametsa, Pärnu Airport – EPU

Tallinn/Ülemiste, Tallinn Airport – TLL

Tartu/Reola, Tartu-Ülenurme Airport – TAY

FINLAND

Enontekiö Airport – ENF

Helsinki-Vantaa Airport – HEL

Ivalo/Inari, Ivalo Airport – IVL

Joensuu/Liperi, Joensuu Airport – JOE

Jyväskylä/Tikkakoski, Jyväskylä Airport – JYV

Kajaani Airport – KAJ

Kemi-Torino Airport – KEM

Kittilä Airport – KTT

Kokkola/Kronoby, Kokkola-Pietarsaari Airport – KOK

Kuopio/Siilinjärvi, Kuopio Airport – KUO

Kuusamo Airport – KAO

Lappeenranta Airport – MHQ

Mariehamm Airport – MHQ

Oulu Airport – OUL

Rovaniemi Airport – RVN

Savonlinna Airport – SVL

Tampere-Pirkkala Airport – TMP

Turku Airport – TKU

Vaasa Airport – VAA

FRANCE

Nice Côte d'Azur Airport – NCE

Carcassonne/Salvaza Airport – CCF

Rodez/Marcillac Airport – RDZ

Marseille/Marignane, Merseille Provence Airport – MRS

Caen/Carpiquet Airport – CFR

Aurillac Airport – AUR

Agoulême/Brie/Champniers Airport – ANG

La Rochelle/Île de Ré Airport – LRH

Brive/Souillac Airport – BE

Ajaccio/Campo dell'Oro, Ajaccio-Napoléon
Bonaparte Airport – AJA

Figari Sud-Corse Airport – FSC

Bastia/Poretta Airport – BIA

Calvi/Sainte-Catherine Airport – CLY

Lannion, Côte de Granit Airport – LAI

Saint-Brieuc/Armor Airport – SBK

Bergerac/Roumanière, Bergerac Dordogne
Périgord Airport – EGC

Périgueux/Bassillac Airport – PGX

Brest/Guipavas, Brest Bretagne Airport – BES

Quimper/Plugaffan, Quimper-Cornouaille Airport –
UIP

Nîmes/Garons, Nîmes-Alès-Camargue-Cévennes Airport – FNI

Toulouse/Blagnac Airport – TLS

Bordeaux/Mérignac Airport – BOD

Bézieres/Vias, Bézieres Cap d'Agde Airport – BZR

Montpellier/Méditerranée Airport – MPL

Dinard/Pleurtuit/Saint-Malo Airport – DNR

Rennes/Saint-Jacques Airport – RNS

Tours/Loire Valley, Tours Val de Loire Airport – TUF

Dole/Tavaux, Dole-Jura Airport – DLE

Saint-Étienne/Bouthéon Airport – EBU

Le Puy/Lourdes Airport – LPY

Nantes/Bouguenais, Nates Atlantique Airport – NTE

Agen, La Garenne Aerodrome – AGF

Angers/Marcé, Angers-Loire Airport – ANE

Cherbourg/Maupertus Airport – CER

Lorient/Lann/Bihoué, Lorient South Brittany Airport – LRT

Metz/Nancy/Lorraine Airport – ETZ

Beauvais/Tillé Airport – BVA

Le Tourquet, Côte d'Opale Airport – LTQ

Clermont-Ferrand/Avurgne Airport – CFE

Biarritz/Pays Basque Airport – BIQ

Pau/Pyrenees Airport – PUF

Tabres-Lourdes-Pyrénées Airport – LDE

Perpigan-Rivesaltes Airport – PGF

Strasbourg/Entzheim, Strasbourg Airport – SXB

Bâle/Mulhouse, EuroAirport Basel-Mulhouse-Freiburg – MLH

Lyon/Saint Exupéry Airport – LYS

Villefranche/Tarare Airport – XVF

Chambéry/Aix-les-Bains, Savoie Airport – CMF

Annecy/Meythet, Annecy-Haute-Savoie-Mont Blanc Airport – NCY

Le Havre/Octeville Airport – LEH

Rouen Airport – URO

Castres/Mazamat Airport – DCM

Troulon/Hyères Airport – TLN

Avignon-Caumont Airport – AVN

Île d'Yeu Aerodrome – IDY

Poitieres-Biard Airport – PIS

Limognes-Bellegarde Airport – LIG

Épinal-Minecourt Airport – EPL

Paris, Charles de Gaulle Airport – CDG

GEORGIA

Batumi International Airport – BUS

Kutaisi International Airport – KUT

Tbilisi International Airport – TBS

GERMANY

Karlsruhe/Baden Baden Airport – FKB

Berlin Tegel Airport – TXL

Berlin Brandenburg Airport – BER

Berlin Schönefeld Airport – SXF

Borkum Airfield – BMK

Bremen Airport – BRE

Cologne/Bonn Airport – CGN

Cuxhaven/Nordholz, Sea-Airport
Cuxhaven/Nordholz – FCN

Dortmund Airport – DTM

Dresden/Klotzsche, Dresden Airport – DRS

Düsseldorf Airport – DUS

Emden Airport – EME

Erfurt, Weimar Airport – ERF

Frankfurt am Main, Frankfurt Airport – FRA

Friedrichshafen Airport – FDH

Hamburg/Fuhlsbüttel, Hamburg Airport – HAM

Hannover Airport – HAJ

Heide, Büsum Airport – HEI

Heligoland/Düne, Heligoland Airport – HGL

Heringsdorf Airport – HDF

Kassel Airport – KSF

Leipzig, Halle Airport – LEJ

Mannheim City Airport – MHG

Memmingen/Allgäu, Memmingen Airport – FMM

Münster-Osnabrück International Airport – FMO

Nuremberg Airport – NUE

Paderborn-Lippstadt Airport – PAD

Rostock, Laage Airport – RLG

Saarbrüken Airport – SCN

Stuttgart Airport – STR

Wangerooge Airfield – AGE

Westerland/Sylt, Sylt Airport – GWT

GREECE

Alexandroupolis International Airport – AXD

Athens/Sparta, Athens International Airport – ATH

Chania International Airport – CHQ

Corfu Island International Airport – CFU

Heraklion International Airport – HER

Kalamata International Airport – KLX

Kavala/Chrysoupoli, Kavala International Airport – KVA

Kefalonia Island International Airport – EFL

Kos Island International Airport – KGS

Lemnos Island International Airport – LXS

Mytilene/Lesbos, Mytilene Island International Airport – MJT

Rhodes Island International Airport – RHO

Samos Island International Airport – SMI

Thessaloniki/Mikra, Thessaloniki International Airport – SKG

Zakynthos Island International Airport – ZTH

HUNGARY

Budapest, Ferenc Liszt International Airport – BUD

Debrecen International Airport – DEB

Sármellék, Hévíz-Balaton Airport – SOB

Gyõr-Pér International Airport – QGY

Pécs-Pogány International Airport – PEV

ICELAND

Akureyri Airport – AEY

Bíldudalur Airport – BIU

Egilsstaðir Airport – EGS

Gjögur Airport – GJR

Grímsey Airport – GRY

Höfn, Hornafjörður Airport – HFN

Húsavík Airport – HZK

Ísafjörður Airport – IFJ

Keflavik International Airport – KEF

Reykjavik Airport – RKV

Sauðárkrókur Airport – SAK

Þórshöfn Airport – THO

Vestmannaeyjar Airport – VEY

Vopnafjörður Airport – VPN

IRELAND

Cork Airport – ORK

Donegal/Dungloe, Donegal Airport – CFN

Dublin Airport – DUB

Kerry Airport – KIR

Knock/Charlestown, Ireland West Airport Knock – NOC

Shannon Airport – SNN

ITALY

Pescara, Abruzzo Airport – PSR

Aosta Valley Airport – AOT

Brindisi/Salento, Brindisi Airport – BDS

Foggia "Gino Lisa" Airport – FOG

Crotone-Sant'Anna Airport – CRV

Lamezia Terme/Catanzaro, Lamezia Terme Airport – SUF

Reggio Calabria "Tito Minniti" Airport – REG

Naples International Airport – NAP

Salerno Costa d'Amalfi Airport – QSR

Bologna Guglielmo Marconi Airport – BLQ

Forlí International Airport – FRL

Parma Airport – PMF

Rimimi, Fedrico Fellini International Airport – RMI

Trieste, Friuli Venezia Giulia Airport – TRS

Rome-Fiumichino International Airport – FCO

Albenga/Savona, Riviera Airport – ALL

Genoa, Cristoforo Colombo Airport – GOA

Bergamo, Bergamo-Orio al Serio Il Caravaggio Airport – BGY

Brescia, Gabriele D'Annunzio Airport – VBS

Milan, Milan Malpensa Airport – MXP

Cuneo International Airport – CUF

Turin Airport – TRN

Alghero, Riviera del Corallo Airport – AHO

Cagliari Elmas Airport – CAG

Olibia, Costa Smeralda Airport – OLB

Tortolí Airport – TTB

Catania-Fontanarossa Airport – CTA

Cosmio Airport – CIY

Lampedusa Airport – LMP

Palermo, Falcone Borsellino Airport - PMO

Panteleria Airport – PNL

Tripani, Vincenzo Florio Airport – TPS

Bolzano Airport – BZO

Florence Airport, Peretola – FLR

Grosseto Airport – GRS

Marina di Campo Airport – EBA

Pisa International Airport – PSA

Perugia, San Francesco d'Assisi-Umbria International Airport – PEG

Treviso Airport – TSP

Venice, Marco Polo Airport – VCE

Verona, Villafranca Airport – VRN

KOSOVO

Pristina International Airport – PRN

LATVIA

Liepaja International Airport – LPX

Riga International Airport – RIX

Ventspils International Airport – VNT

LITHUANIA

Kaunas International Airport – KUN

Palanga International Airport – PLQ

Šiauliai International Airport – SQQ

Vilnius International Airport – VNO

LUXEMBOURG

Luxembourg Airport – LUX

MALTA

Luqa, Malta International Airport – MLA

MOLDOVA

Chisinau International Airport – KIV

MONTENEGRO

Podgorica Airport – TGD

Tivat Airport – TIV

NETHERLANDS

Amsterdam/Haarlemmermeer, Amsterdam Airport Schipol – AMS

Eindhoven Airport – EIN

Groningen Airport Eelde – GRQ

Maastricht Aachen Airport – MST

Rotterdam The Hague Airport – RTM

NORTH MACEDONIA

Ohrid, St. Paul the Apostle Airport – OHD

Skopje International Airport – SKP

NORWAY

Ålesund Airport, Vigra – AES

Alta Airport – ALF

Andøya Airport, Andenes – ANX

Bardufoss Airport – BDU

Båtsfjord Airport – BJF

Bergen Airport, Flesland – BGO

Berlevåg Airport – BVG

Bodø Airport – BOO

Brønnøysund Airport, Brønnøy – BNN

Florø Airport – FRO

Førde Airport, Bringeland – FDE

Hammerfest Airport – HFT

Harstad/Narvik Airport, Evenes – EVE

Hasvik Airport – HAA

Haugesund Airport, Karmøy – HAU

Honningsvåg Airport, Valan – HVG

Kirkenes Airport, Høybuktmoen – KKN

Kristiansund Airport, Kjevik - KRS

Kristiansund Airport, Kvernberget – KSU

Lakselv Airport, Banak – LKL

Leknes Airport – LKN

Mehamn Airport – MEH

Mo i Rana Airport, Røssvoll – MQN

Molde Airport, Årø – MOL

Mosjøen Airport, Kjærstad – MJF

Namsos Airport, Høknesøra – OSY

Notodden Airport, Tuven – NTB

Brekstad, Ørland Airport – OLA

Ørsta-Volda Airport, Hovden – HOV

Oslo Airport, Gardermoen – OSL

Røros Airport – RRS

Rørvik Airport, Ryum – RVK

Røst Airport – RET

Sandane Airport, Anda – SDN

Sandefjord Airport, Torp – TRF

Sandnessjøen Airport, Stokka – SSJ

Sogndal Airport, Haukåsen – SOG

Sørkjosen Airport – SOJ

Stavanger Airport, Sola – SVG

Stokmarknes Airport, Skagen – SKN

Leirvik, Stord Airport, Sørstokken- SRP

Longyearbyen, Svalbard Airport, Longyear – LYR

Svolvær Airport, Helle – SVJ

Tromsø Airport – TOS

Trondheim Airport, Værnes – TRD

Vadsø Airport – VDS

Vardø Airport, Svartnes – VAW

POLAND

Warsaw Chopin Airport – WAW

Kraków, John Paul II International Airport – KRK

Gdansk, Lech Wałesa Airport – GDN

Katowice Airport – KTW

Wrocław, Copernicus Airport – WRO

Poznan-Ławica Henryk Wieniawski Airport – POZ

Rzeszów-Jasonika Airport – RZE

Szczecin, Solidaridy Szczecin-Goleniów Airport – SZZ

Lublin Airport – LUZ

Bydgoszcz, Ignacy Jan Paderewski Airport – BZG

Łódz, Władysław Reymont Airport – LCJ

Olsztyn-Mazury Airport – SZY

Zielona Góra Airport – IEG

PORTUGAL

Beja Airport – BYJ

Braga Airport – BGZ

Bragança Airport – BGC

Cascias, Lisbon Cascias-Tejo Regional Airport – LCT

Chaves Airport – CHV

Coimbra Airport – CBP

Faro Airport – FAO

Lisbon Airport – LIS

Portimao Airport – PRM

Porto, Francisco Sá Carneiro Airport – OPO

Vila Riel Airport – VRL

Viseu Airport – VSE

ROMANIA

Bacau, George Enescu International Airport – BCM

Baia Mare/Tautii-Magheraus, Maramures International Airport – BAY

Bucharest, Henri Coanda International Airport – OTP

Cluj-Napoca, Avram Iancu Cluj International Airport – CLJ

Constanta, Mihail Kogalniceanu Airport – CND

Craiova International Airport – CRA

Iasi International Airport – IAS

Oradea Airport – OMR

Satu Mare Airport – SUJ

Sibiu International Airport – SBZ

Suceava, Stefan cel Mare International Airport – SCV

Târgu Mures, Transilvania Airport – TGM

Timisoara, Traian Vuia International Airport – TSR

SERBIA

Belgrade, Nikola Tesla Airport – BEG

Nis, Constantine the Great Airport – INI

SLOVAKIA

Bratislava, M. R. Štefánik Airport – BTS

Košice International Airport – KSC

SLOVENIA

Ljubljana, Jože Pucnik Airport – LJU

SPAIN

A Coruña Airport – LCG

Albacete Airport – ABC

Alicante-Elche Airport – ALC

Almería Airport – LEI

Asturias Airport – OVD

Badajoz Airport – BJZ

Barcelona, El Prat Josep Tarradellas Airport – BCN

Bilbao Airport – BIO

Burgos Airport – RGS

Córdoba Airport – ODB

Castellón Airport – CDT

Girona-Costa Brava Airport – GRO

Granada/Jaén, Federico García Lorca
Airport – GRX

Huesca, Pirineos Airport – HSK

Jerez de la Frontera, Jerez Airport – XRY

Andorra/La Seu d'Urgell Airport – LEU

León Airport – LEN

Lleida-Alguaire Airport – ILD

Logroño-Agoncillo Airport – RJL

Madrid-Barajas Airport – MAD

Málaga Airport – AGP

Pamplona-Nóain Airport – PNA

Región de Murcia International Airport –
RMU

Reus Airport – REU

Salamanca Airport – SLM

San Sebastián Airport – EAS

Santander Airport – SDR

Santiago de Compostela Airport – SDR

Seville Airport – SVQ

Teruel Airport – TEV

Valencia Airport – VLC

Valladolid Airport – VLL

Vigo Airport – VGO

Vitoria Airport – VIT

Zaragoza Airport – ZAZ

SWEDEN

Arvidsjaur Airport – AJR

Borlänge Airport – BLE

Gothenburg, Göteborg Landvetter Airport – GOT

Gällivare Airport – GEV

Hagfors Airport – HFS

Halmstad City Airport – HAD

Hemavan Airport – HMV

Jönköping Airport – JKG

Kalmar Airport – KLR

Karlstad Airport – KSD

Kiruna Airport – KRN

Kramfors, Höga Kusten Airport – KRF

Kristianstad Airport – KID

Linköping/Saab Airport – LPI

Luleå Airport – LLA

Lycksele Airport – LYC

Malmö Airport – MMX

Mora-Siljan Airport – MXX

Norrköping Airport – NRK

Pajala Airport – PJA

Ronneby Airport – RNB

Skellefteå Airport – SFT

Stockholm Arlanda Airport – ARN

Sundsvall-Timrå Airport – SDL

Sveg Airport – EVG

Torsby Airport – TYF

Trollhättan-Vänersborg Airport – THN

Umeå Airport – UME

Vihelmina Airport – VHM

Visby Airport – VBY

Växjö/Kronoberg Airport – VXO

Ängelholm/Helsingborg Airport – AGH

Örebro Airport – ORB

Örnsköldsvik Airport – OER

Are Östersund Airport – OSD

SWITZERLAND

Basel, EuroAirport Basel Mulhouse Freiburg – BSL

Bern/Belp, Regional Aerodrome Bern-Belp – BRN

Geneva Airport – GVA

Lugano Airport – LUG

Sion Airport – SIR

St. Gallen/Altenrhein Airport – ACH

Zurich Airport – ZRH

TURKEY

Adana Airport – ADA

Ankara Esenboga Airport – ESB

Alanya, Gazipasa Airport – GZP

Antalya Airport – AYT

Balıkesir Koca Seyit Airport – EDO

Bursa Yenisehir Airport – YEI

Denizli Çardak Airport – DNZ

Diyarbakır Airport – DIY

Elazıg Airport – EZS

Erzurum Airport – ERZ

Eskisehir, Hasan Polatkan Airport – AOE

Gaziantep Airport – GZT

Hatay Airport – HTY

Isparta, Süleyman Demirel Airport – ISE

Istanbul Airport – IST

İzmir Adnan Menderes Airport – ADB

Kars Harakani Airport – KSY

Kayseri Airport – ASR

Kocaeli Cengiz Topel Airport – KCO

Konya Airport – KYA

Kütahya, Zafer Airport – KZR

Malatya Airport – MLX

Mugla, Milas-Bodrum Airport – BJV

Nevsehir Kapadokya Airport – NAV

Ordu Giresun Airport – OGU

Samsun-Çarsamba Airport – SZF

Sinop Airport – NOP

Sivas Nuri Demirag Airport – VAS

Sanlıurfa GAP Airport – GNY

Tekirdag Çorlu Airport – TEQ

Trabzon Airport – TZX

Van, Ferit Melen Airport – VAN

Zonguldak Çaycuma Airport – ONQ

UKRAINE

Kiev, Boryspil International Airport – KBP

Chernivtsi International Airport – CWC

Dnipro, Dnipropetrovsk International Airport – DNK

Ivano-Frankivsk International Airport – IFO

Kharkiv International Airport – HRK

Kherson International Airport – KHE

Kryvyi Rih International Airport – KWG

Lviv Danylo Halytskyi International Airport – LWO

Odessa International Airport – ODS

Rivne International Airport – RWN

Vinnytsia Airport – VIN

Zaporizhia International Airport – OZH

UNITED KINGDOM

England

Castle Donington, East Midlands Airport – EMA

Luton Airport – LTN

Norwich Airport – NWI

Southend, London Southend Airport – SEN

Stansted Airport – STN

London, Heathrow Airport

Woolsington, Newcastle Airport – NCL

Liverpool John Lennon Airport – LPL

Ringway, Manchester Airport – MAN

Crawley, Gatwick Airport – LGW

Southampton Airport – SOU

Clyst Honiton, Exeter Airport – EXT

Hurn, Bournemouth Airport – BOH

Mawgan in Pydar, Newquay Airport – NQY

St. Just, Land's End Airport – LEQ

St. Mary's Airport – ISC

Lulsgate, Bristol Airport – BRS

Solihull, Birmingham Airport – BHX

Finningley, Doncaster Sheffield Airport – DSA

Kirmington, Humberside Airport – HUY

Leeds Bradford International Airport – LBA

Northern Ireland

Aldergrove, Belfast International Airport – BFS

Eglinton, City of Derry Airport – LDY

Scotland

Aberdeen International Airport – ABZ

Ardchattan, Oban Airport – OBN

Benbecula Airport – BEB

Barra Airport – BRR

Campbeltown Airport – CAL

Coll Airport – COL

Colonsay Airport – CSA

North Ronaldsay Airport – NRL

Delcross, Inverness Airport – INV

Dundee Airport – DND

Dunrossness, Sumburgh Airport – LSI

Eday Airport – EOI

Edinburgh Airport – EDI

Fair Isle Airport – FIE

Islay Airport – ILY

Sanday Airport – NDY

Papa Stour Airport – PSV

Papa Westray Airport – PPW

Paisley, Glasgow International Airport – GLA

Stornoway Airport – SYY

Stronsay Airport – SOY

Tingwall Airport – LWK

Tiree Airport – TRE

Westray Airport – WRY

Wick Airport – WIC

Wales

Llanfair yn Neubwll, Anglesey Airport – VLY

Rhoose, Cardiff Airport – CWF

Guernsey

Alderney Airport – ACI

Isle of Man

Malew, Isle of Man Public Airport – IOM

Jersey

St. Peter, Jersey Airport – JER

Oceania

AUSTRALIA

Australian Capital Territory

Canberra Airport – CBR

New South Wales

Albury Airport – ABX

Armidale Airport – ARM

Ballina, Ballina Byron Gateway Airport – BNK

Bathurst Airport – BHS

Broken Hill Airport – BHQ

Cobar Airport – CAZ

Coffs Harbour Airport – CFS

Cooma, Snowy Mountains Airport – OOM

Dubbo City Airport – DBO

Grafton/Clarence Valley, Clarence Valley Regional Airport – GFN

Griffith Airport – GFF

Lismore Airport – LSY

Lord Howe Island Airport – LDH

Merimbula Airport – MIM

Moree Airport – MRZ

Moruya Airport – MYA

Mudgee Airport – DGE

Narrabri Airport – NAA

Narrandera Airport – NRA

Newcastle Airport – NTL

Orange Airport – OAG

Parkes Airport – PKE

Port Macquarie Airport – PQQ

Sydney Airport – SYD

Tamworth Airport – TMW

Taree Airport – TRO

Wagga Wagga Airport – WGA

Wollongong, Illawara Regional Airport – WOL

Northern Territory

Alice Springs Airport – ASP

Croker Island Airport – CKI

Darwin International Airport – DRW

Elcho Island Airport – ELC

Gapuwiyak, Lake Evella Airport – LEL

Goulburn Islands, South Goulburn Island Airport – GBL

The Granites Airport – GTS

Groote Eylandt Airport – GTE

Maningrida Airport – MNG

Milikapiti, Snake Bay Airport – SNB

Milingimbi Airport – MGT

Ngukurr Airport – RPM

Nhulunbuy, Gove Airport

Ramingining Airport – RAM

Tennant Creek Airport – TCA

Uluru, Ayers Rock Airport – AYQ

Queensland

Aurukun Airport – AUU

Bamaga, Northern Peninsula Airport – ABM

Barcaldine Airport – BCI

Bedourie Airport – BEU

Birdsville Airport – BVI

Blackall Airport – BKQ

Boulia Airport – BQL

Brisbane Airport – BNE

Bundaberg Airport – BDB

Burketown Airport – BUC

Cairns Airport – CNS

Charleville Airport – CTL

Cloncurry Airport – CNJ

Coconut Island Airport – CNC

Cooktown Airport – CTN

Cunnamulla Airport – CMA

Darnley Island Airport – NLF

Doomadgee Airport – DMD

Emerald Airport – EMD

Gladstone Airport – GLT

Gold Coast Airport – OOL

Hamilton Island, Great Barrier Reef Airport – HTI

Hervey Bay Airport – HVB

Horn Island Airport – HID

Hughenden Airport – HGD

Julia Creek Airport – JCK

Karumba Airport – KRB

Kubin Airport – KUG

Lizard Island Airport – LZR

Lockhart River Airport – IRG

Longreach Airport – LRE

Mabuiag Island Airport – UBB

Mackay Airport – MKY

Marcoola, Sunshine Coast Airport – MCY

Moranbah Airport – MOV

Mornington Island Airport – ONG

Mount Isa Airport – ISA

Murray Island Airport – MYI

Normanton Airport – NTN

Palm Island Airport – PMK

Pormpuraaw, Edward River Airport – EDR

Proserpine, Whitsunday Coast Airport – PPP

Quilpie Airport – ULP

Richmond Airport – RCM

Rockhampton Airport – ROK

Roma Airport – RMA

Saibai Island Airport – SBR

St. George Airport – SGO

Sue Islet, Warraber Island Airport – SYU

Thangool Airport – THG

Thargomindah Airport – XTG

Toowoomba Wellcamp Airport – WTB

Townsville Airport – TSV

Weipa Airport – WEI

Windorah Airport – WNR

Winton Airport – WIN

Yam Island Airport – XMY

Yorke Island Airport – OKR

South Australia

Adelaide Airport – ADL

Ceduna Airport – CED

Coober Perdy Airport – CPD

Kingscote/Kangaroo Island – Kingscote Airport – KGC

Leigh Creek Airport – LGH

Moomba Airport – MOO

Mount Gambier Airport – MGB

Olympic Dam Airport – OLP

Port Augusta Airport – PUG

Port Lincoln Airport – PLO

Prominent Hill Airport – PXH

Whyalla Airport – WAY

Tasmania

Devonport Airport – DPO

Flinders Island Airport – FLS

Hobart International Airport – HBA

Launceston Airport – LST

Wynyard, Burnie Airport – BWT

Victoria

Avalon Airport – AVV

Melbourne Airport – MEL

Mildura Airport – MQL

Portland Airport – PTJ

Warrnambool Airport – WMB

Western Australia

Albany Airport – ALH

Boolgeeda Airport – OCM

Broome International Airport – BME

Carnarvon Airport – CVQ

Esperance Airport – EPR

Exmouth, Learmouth Airport – LEA

Fitzroy Crossing Airport – FIZ

Geraldton Airport – GET

Halls Creek Airport – HCQ

Kalbarri Airport – KAX

Kalgoorlie-Boulder Airport – KGI

Karratha Airport – KTA

Kununurra Airport – KNX

Laverton Airport – LVO

Leinster Airport – LER

Leonora Airport – LNO

Monkey Mia, Shark Bay Airport – MJK

Mount Magnet Airport – MMG

Newman Airport – ZNE

Onslow Airport – ONS

Paraburdoo Airport – PBO

Perth Airport – PER

Port Hedland International Airport – PHE

Rottnest Island Airport – RTS

Willuna Airport – WUN

Christmas Island

Christmas Island Airport – XCH

Cocos (Keeling) Islands

Cocos (Keeling) Islands Airport – CCK

Norfolk Island

Norfolk Island Airport – NLK

FIJI

Nadi International Airport – NAN

Nausori/Suva, Nausori International Airport – SUV

Cicia Airport – ICI

Gau Airport – NGI

Koro Airport – KXF

Labasa Airport – LBS

Lakeba Airport – LKB

Levuka Airfield – LEV

Malolo Lailai Airport – PTF

Mana Island Airport – MNF

Matei Airport – TVU

Moala Airport – MFJ

Rotuma Airport – RTA

Savusavu Airport – SVU

Vanuabalavu Airport – VBV

Vunisea Airport – KDV

Yasawa Island Airport – YAS

KIRIBATI

Kiritimati, Cassidy International Airport – CXI

Tarawa, Bonriki International Airport – TRW

Abaiang, Abaiang Atoll Airport – ABF

Abemama, Abemama Atoll Airport – AEA

Aranuka Airport – AAK

Arorae Island Airport – AIS

Beru Island Airport – BEZ

Butaritari Atoll Airport – BBG

Marakei Airport – MZK

Nikunau Airport – NIG

MARSHALL ISLANDS

Ailinglaplap Airok Airport – AIC

Jeh Airport – JEJ

Woja Airport – WJA

Ailuk Airport – AIM

Ine Airport – IMI

Tinak Airport – TIC

Aur Airport – AUL

Bikini Atoll Airport – BII

Ebon Airport – EBO

Jabot Airport – JAT

Jaluit Airport – UIT

Kili Airport – KIO

Ebadon Airstrip – EBN

Elenak Airport – EAL

Lae Airport – LML

Likiep Airport – LIK

Majuro, Marshall Islands International Airport – MAJ

Kaben Airport – KBT

Taroa Island, Maloelap Airport – MAV

Mejit Airport – MJB

Enejit Airport – EJT

Mili Airport – MIJ

Namdrik Airport – NDK

Majkin Airport – MJE

Ronjelap Airport – RNP

Ujae Airport – UJE

Utirik Airport – UTK

Wotho Airport – WTO

Wotje Airport – WTE

MICRONESIA

Chuuk International Airport – TKK

Kosrae International Airport – KSA

Pohnpei International Airport – PNI

Ulithi Airport – ULI

Yap International Airport – YAP

NAURU

Nauru International Airport – INU

NEW ZEALAND

Aukland Airport – AKL

Bienheim Airport – BHE

Catham Islands/Tuuta Airport – CHT

Christchurch International Airport – CHC

Dunedin International Airport – DUD

Gisborne Airport – GIS

Great Barrier Aerodrome - GBZ

Hamilton Airport – HLZ

Hokitika Airport – HKK

Invercargill Airport – IVC

Kaikoura Aerodrome – KBZ

Kaitaia Airport – KAT

Kerikeri Airport – KKE

Masterton, Hood Aerodrome – MRO

Mount Cook Aerodrome – MON

Napier/Hastings, Napier Airport – NPE

Nelson Airport – NSN

New Plymouth Airport – NPL

Oamaru Airport – OAM

Palmerson North Airport – PMR

Paraparaumu, Kapiti Coast Airport – PPQ

Picton Aerodrome – PCN

Queenstown International Airport – ZQN

Rotorua Airport – ROT

Wellington International Airport – WLG

Westport Airport – WSZ

Whahatane Airport – WHK

Whanganui Airport – WAG

Whangarei Airport – WRE

Whitianga Aerodrome - WTZ

PALAU

Babeldaob Island, Roman Tmetuchl International Airport – ROR

PAPUA NEW GUINEA

Alotau, Gurney Airport – GUR

Buka Airport – BUA

Bulolo Airport – BUL

Daru Airport – DAU

Efogi Airport – EFG

Goroka Airport – GKA

Hoskins Airport – HKN

Kavieng Airport – KVG

Kerema Airport – KMA

Kikori Airport – KRI

Kiunga Airport – UNG

Kokoda Airport – KKD

Kundiawa, Chimbu Airport – CMU

Lae, Lae Nadzab Airport – LAE

Lake Murray Airport – LMY

Lorengau, Momote Airport – MAS

Louisia Airport – LSA

Madang Airport – MAG

Mendi Airport – MDU

Misima Airport – MIS

Mount Hagen Airport – HGU

Girua Airport – PNP

Port Moresby, Jacksons International Airport – POM

Rabaul/Kokopo, Tokua Airport – RAB

Tabubil Airport – TBG

Tari Airport – TIZ

Tufi Airport – TFI

Vanimo Airport – VAI

Wanigela Airport – AGL

Wewak Airport – WWK

SAMOA

Apia, Faleolo International Airport – APW

Asau Airport – AAU

Fagali'i Airport – FGI

SOLOMON ISLANDS

Akui Gwaunaru'u Airport – AKS

Balale Airport – BAS

Choiseul Bay Airport – CHY

Gizo, Nusatupe Airport – GZO

Honiara International Airport – HIR

Kirakira Airport – IRA

Mono Airport – MNY

Munda Airport – MUA

Ramata Airport – RBV

Tingoa, Rennel/Tingoa Airport – RNL

Santa Ana Airport – NNB

Santa Cruz Islands, Santa Cruz/Graciosa Bay/Luova Airport – SCZ

Seghe Airport – EGM

Yandina Airport – XYA

TONGA

'Eua Airport – EUA

Lifuka/Ha'apai, Lifuka Island Airport – HPA

Niuafo'ou Airport – NFO

Niutoputapu Airport – NTT

Nuku'Alofa, Fua'amotu International Airport – TBU

Vava'u International Airport – VAV

TUVALU

Funafuti International Airport – FUN

VANUATU

Anatom/Inyueg, Anatom Airport – AUY

Aniwa Airport – AWD

Craig Cove Airport – CCV

Dillon's Bay Airport – DLY

Sangafa, Siwo Airport - EAE

Futuna Airport – FTA

Gaua Airport – ZGU

Ipota Airport – IPA

Lamap/Malekula, Malekula Airport – LPM

Lamen Bay Airport – LNB

Longana Airport – LOD

Lonorore Airport – LNE

Luganville, Santo-Pekoa Internaational Airport – SON

Maewo, Maewo-Naone Airport – MWF

Mota Lava Airport – MTV

Norsup Airport – NUS

Olpoi Airport – OLJ

Tavie, Paama Airport – PBJ

Port Vila, Bauerfield International Airport – VLI

Redcliffe Airport – RCL

Sara Airport – SSR

Sola, Vanua Lava Airport – SLH

South West Bay Airport – SWJ

Whitegrass Airport – TAH

Tongoa Airport – TGH

Linua, Torres Airport – TOH

Ulei Airport – ULB

Valesdir Airport – VLS

Walaha Airport – WLH

Dependant Territories of Oceania

AMERICAN SAMOA (USA)

Pago Pago International Airport – PPG

COOK ISLANDS (NEW ZEALAND)

Aitutaki Airport – AIT

Atiu, Enua Airport – AIU

Mangaia Airport – MGS

Manihiki Island Airport – MHX

Mauke Airport – MUK

Mitiaro Airport – MOI

Penrhyn Island, Tongareva Airport – PYE

Rarotonga International Airport – RAR

FRENCH POLYNESIA (FRANCE)

Ahe Airport – AHE

Anaa Airport – AAA

Apataki Airport – APK

Arutua Airport – AXR

Bora Bora Airport – BOB

Fakarava Airport – FAV

Fangatau Airport – FGU

Hao Airport – HOI

Hiva Oa, Atuona Airport – AUQ

Huahine/Fare Airport – HUH

Kaukura Airport – KKR

Makemo Airport – MKP

Manihi Airport – XMH

Matavia Airport – MVT

Maupiti Airport – MAU

Moorea Airport – MOZ

Nuku Hiva Airport – NHV

Puka-Puka Airport – PKP

Raiatea Airport – RFP

Rangiroa Airport – RGI

Reao Airport – REA

Rimatara Airport – RMT

Rurutu Airport – RUR

Tahiti, Faaa International Airport – PPT

Takapoto Airport – TKP

Takaroa Airport – TKX

Tikehau Airport – TIH

Totegegie Airport – GMR

Tubuai, Mataura Airport – TUB

Ua Huka Airport – UAH

Ua Pou Airport – UAP

Vahitahi Airport – VHZ

GUAM (USA)

Agana, Antonio B. Won Pat International Airport – GUM

NEW CALEDONIA (FRANCE)

Île Art-Waala Airport – BMY

Île des Pins Airport – ILP

Koné Airport – KNQ

Koumac Airport – KOC

Lifou Airport – LIF

Maré Airport – MEE

Nouméa Magenta Airport – GEA

Ouvéa Airport – UVE

Tiga Airport – TGJ

Touho Airport – TOU

NIUE (NEW ZEALAND)

Niue International Airport – IUE

NORTHERN MARIANA ISLANDS (USA)

Saipan International Airport – SPN

Rota International Airport – ROP

Tinian International Airport – TIQ

WALLIS & FUTUNA (FRANCE)

Wallis, Hihifo Airport – WLS